Getting Started
with
Elementary School Sentence Composing

Getting Started
with
Elementary
School Sentence
Composing

A Student Worktext

Don and Jenny Killgallon

HEINEMANN
Portsmouth, NH

Heinemann
361 Hanover Street
Portsmouth, NH 03801–3912
www.heinemann.com

Offices and agents throughout the world

The authors and publisher wish to thank those who have generously given permission to reprint borrowed material:

Drawing by Don Killgallon from *Sentence Composing for Elementary School: A Sentence-Composing Approach* by Don and Jenny Killgallon. Copyright © 2000 by Don and Jenny Killgallon. Published by Heinemann. Reprinted by permission of the Publisher. All rights reserved.

Cataloging-in-Publication Data is on file at the Library of Congress.
978-0-325-09230-0

Acquisitions Editor: Tobey Antao
Production Editor: Sean Moreau
Cover and Interior Designer: Monica Ann Crigler
Typesetter: Valerie Levy, Drawing Board Studios
Manufacturing: Steve Bernier

Printed in the United States of America on acid-free paper

1 2 3 4 5 6 7 8 9 10 RWP 25 24 23 22 21 20

March 2020 Printing

To Tobey Antao, our constant editor, for her sight:
foresight, hindsight, oversight, insight—all with 20/20 vision.

CONTENTS

This book will help you build better sentences like those of authors. You will learn how to use their sentence-composing tools to write more skillfully.

QUICKSHOTS FOR NEW WORDS 1

Inside, you'll meet new words, but you'll get instant help to learn what they mean. A quickshot is a familiar word placed right next to an unknown word to keep you reading smoothly.

BASIC SENTENCE TRAINING

Before learning how to build better sentences, you need to know what a sentence is, what its parts are, and what tools good writers use to build strong sentences.

SUBJECTS AND PREDICATES 6

SENTENCE-COMPOSING TOOLS 21

REPAIRING BROKEN SENTENCES

Sentence parts are not complete sentences. If a sentence *part* begins with a capital letter and ends with a period, it is a broken sentence, just a piece of a sentence called a fragment. In this section you'll learn to spot and repair broken sentences and avoid them in your writing.

FRAGMENTS 37

LEARNING BY IMITATING

STARTING SENTENCE IMITATING   45

To learn how to do something, imitate people who know how. To learn to build your own strong sentences, you'll imitate how authors build their sentences.

PRACTICING SENTENCE IMITATING   55

Doing these activities, you'll practice building sentences like those of published authors.

THE SENTENCE-COMPOSING TOOLS

USING SENTENCE-COMPOSING TOOLS   72

Just as power tools make building a good house easier, sentence-composing tools make building a strong sentence easier.

THE TOOLBOX   87

To get the job done right in your sentences, use the right tools in the right places. You've learned all of the right parts to build stronger sentences: subjects, predicates, tools. Those power sentence-composing parts are in your toolbox. Get ready to use them in this section. When you finish, admire your work, done right with the right parts, and take a bow.

THE SENTENCE-COMPOSING APPROACH

Nothing is more satisfying than to write a good sentence.

—Barbara Tuchman, historian

QUICKSHOTS FOR NEW WORDS

When we're just getting to know a word, or when a word is completely new to us, it can be a help to see the word in a sentence. For example, take a look at the following words. Some of these words might feel familiar to you, while others might be unfamiliar:

- quality

- longevity

- adversity

- ignorance

- bliss

- folly

- err

- divine

- moral

- immoral

How did that list look to you? Were there some words you knew? Were there some words you didn't know?

Now, let's take a look at those same words again. This time, let's look at them in a sentence.

1. The **quality**, not the **longevity**, of a person's life is what is important.
   —Martin Luther King Jr.

2. Sweet are the uses of **adversity**.
   —William Shakespeare

3. Where **ignorance** is **bliss**, it is **folly** to be wise.

—Thomas Gray

4. To **err** is human, but to forgive is **divine**.

—Alexander Pope (adapted)

5. There's no **moral** way to approve very **immoral** actions.

—Rudolph Giuliani

Did having context help you with the meanings of any of those words? It might—or it might not. You've probably seen that context can be helpful, but it doesn't guarantee that the meaning of the word will become clear.

In this worktext, help is on the way. Like the words in those sentences, some words in this worktext may be unfamiliar. For those, you'll see a quickshot definition **alongside** [*beside*] the bolded unfamiliar word. (You just saw your first quickshot.)

Here's an example. Read this sentence by Rudolph Giuliani, then mayor of New York City, in his speech to the General Assembly of the United Nations on October 1, 2001, condemning the tragedy of terrorist attacks in New York and elsewhere on September 11, 2001.

There's no moral way to approve very immoral actions.

The meaning of the sentence is roughly this: There's no SOMETHING way to approve very SOMETHING actions.

What way? What actions?

You could take time-out for dictionary diving to find out what *moral* means, and its opposite *immoral*.

Instead, in this worktext you'll get a quicker, easier way called a "quickshot." Throughout this worktext when words are **bold**, a short definition—a quickshot—will be next to it. If you already know the word, just skip ahead. If you don't, a quickshot will get you through the sentence without stumbling.

Here is Mayor Giuliani's sentence with quickshots.

----

*There's no moral [right] way to approve
very immoral [wrong] actions.*

Here is the Mayor's meaning: there's no right way to approve very wrong actions.

Quickshots give a short but not perfect definition. For example, you now know that *moral* means right, *immoral* means wrong, but know also that *moral* and *immoral* refer only to human behavior being right or wrong. If you got most of the words right on a spelling test, you wouldn't say, "I got most spellings moral, but some immoral."

Here are the other sentences, this time with quickshots.

WORDS IN SENTENCES WITH QUICKSHOTS

1. The **quality** [*value*], not the **longevity** [*length*], of a person's life is what is important.
    —Martin Luther King Jr.

    In other words: The value, not the length, of a person's life is what is important. It's not how long a person lives but how well.

2. Sweet are the uses of **adversity** [*problems*].
    —William Shakespeare

    In other words: People can learn from their problems, including ways to avoid those same problems.

3. Where **ignorance** [*not knowing*] is **bliss** [*happiness*], it is **folly** [*foolish*] to be wise.

—Oliver Goldsmith

In other words: Sometimes it's better to not know about disturbing events.

4. To **err** [*make mistakes*] is human, but to forgive is **divine** [*like a god*].

—Alexander Pope

In other words: We all make mistakes, but the good people forgive us.

5. There's no **moral** [*right*] way to approve **very immoral** [*wrong*] actions.

—Rudolph Giuliani

In other words: There's no right way to approve very wrong actions.

QUIZ: QUICKSHOTS

Directions: Select the best meaning for the bolded word.

1. The quality, not the **longevity**, of a person's life is what is important.

   a. health

   b. achievements

   c. length

2. Sweet are the uses of **adversity**.

   a. wisdom

   b. difficulties

   c. desserts

3. Where ignorance is **bliss**, it is **folly** to be wise.

    a. strange / important

    b. happiness / foolish

    c. stupid / smart

4. To **err** is human, but to forgive is **divine**.

    a. talk / silly

    b. make mistakes / godlike

    c. apologize / necessary

5. There's no **moral** way to approve **immoral** actions.

    a. good / bad

    b. certain / hasty

    c. final / wrong

BASIC SENTENCE TRAINING

SUBJECTS AND PREDICATES

A subject is a topic. A predicate is a comment about the topic. A topic is a person, place, or thing. A comment is a remark about that person, place, or thing. For a sentence, you need a subject plus a predicate.

EXAMPLES

SUBJECT (topic):

      a. the kids in Room 207

      b. Chester the cat

      c. most dangerous sharks

      d. the large woman

      e. smoke and flames

PREDICATE (comment about a topic):

      a. were misbehaving again

      b. was curled up on the brown velvet armchair

      c. are the ones that are both hungry and mean

      d. turned around and kicked him right in his blue-jeaned sitter

      e. were pouring out of the spaces where the windows had been

SENTENCE (SUBJECT PLUS PREDICATE): The subject (topic) is underlined once. The predicate (comment about the topic) is underlined twice.

    a. The kids in Room 207 were misbehaving again.

        —Harry Allard, *Miss Nelson Is Missing!*

    b. Chester the cat was curled up on the brown velvet armchair.

        —Deborah and James Howe, *Bunnicula: A Rabbit-Tale of Mystery*

    c. Most dangerous sharks are the ones that are both hungry and mean.

        —Willard Price, *Diving Adventure*

    d. The large woman turned around and kicked him right in his blue-jeaned sitter.

        —Langston Hughes, "Thank You, Ma'am"

    e. Smoke and flames were pouring out of the spaces where the windows had been. (*Comment is about two subjects—smoke and flames.*)

        —Franklin W. Dixon, *The Secret of the Old Mill*

Note: Sentences 1–5 have the same subject but different predicates.

    1. The squirrel in the tree leaped from the branch.

    2. The squirrel in the tree climbed higher.

    3. The squirrel in the tree stood still.

    4. The squirrel in the tree made a clicking sound.

    5. The squirrel in the tree ate an acorn.

Note: Sentences 6–10 have the same predicate but different subjects.

6. <u>The kids who were playing</u> <u>started to sing</u>.

7. <u>Harry, Lisa, and Jamal</u> <u>started to sing</u>.

8. <u>Tiffany during the silence</u> <u>started to sing</u>.

9. <u>Before the beginning of the game, Harriet</u> <u>started to sing</u>.

10. <u>For their performance of the school song, the choir</u> <u>started to sing</u>.

ACTIVITY 1: PUTTING SUBJECTS AND PREDICATES TOGETHER

Directions: Match the subject with its predicate to make a complete sentence.

SUBJECT (topic)	PREDICATE (comment about the topic)
1. The fairy godmother	a. resulted in a win for our school.
2. A locker stuffed with books	b. showed up under the bus seat.
3. The missing book bag	c. turned the mice into horses.
4. Singing the song repeatedly	d. also contained Terry's backpack.
5. The first game of the season	e. helped me remember the lyrics.

ACTIVITY 2: IDENTIFYING SUBJECTS AND PREDICATES

Directions: Is it a subject or a predicate? Remember that a subject is a topic. A predicate is a comment about the topic. Use S for subject, and P for predicate.

1. stumbled over the rock at the end of the path

2. looked out at the pouring rain hitting the road

3. a child in a Halloween costume

4. laughed out loud at his friend's joke

5. the bunny in the rabbit hole in the front yard

6. a detective in a striped suit

7. ran across the street to chase the cat

8. hiccupped repeatedly during the assembly

9. a student new to the school

10. a dark cloud above the stadium

After you identify the subject or the predicate, complete the sentence by adding the missing part. Write out your sentences, underlining the subject once, and predicate twice.

EXAMPLES (Subjects are underlined once, and predicates twice.)

Subject: the cobra in the basket

Sentence: The cobra in the basket rose because of the snake charmer's music.

Predicate: ran onto the curb and startled the driving teacher

Sentence: The student driver ran onto the curb and startled the driving teacher.

ACTIVITY 3: MATCHING

Directions: Match the subject with its predicate to make a sentence. Write out each sentence.

SUBJECT (topic)

1. A board ^ .
   > —Thomas Rockwell, *How to Eat Fried Worms*

2. A deeper fog ^ .
   > —Barbara Brooks Wallace, *Peppermints in the Parlor*

3. A whirl of bats frightened from slumber by their smoking torches ^ .
   > —J. R. R. Tolkien, *The Hobbit*

4. Her legs and arms ^ .
   > —Madeleine L'Engle, *A Wrinkle in Time*

5. A wild-eyed horse with its bridle torn and dangling, ^ .
   > —Lois Lowry, *The Giver*

PREDICATE (comment about the topic)

a. were tingling faintly as though they had been asleep

b. trotted frantically through the mounds of men, tossing its head, whinnying in panic

c. began to creep stealthily up from the sea, spreading over San Francisco to dim the lights of its buildings and to turn them into monstrous shadows

d. creaked on the stairs

e. flew over the dwarves

ACTIVITY 4: PUTTING HARRY POTTER SENTENCES TOGETHER

Directions: Using the following sentences from J. K. Rowling's Harry Potter stories, match the subject with its predicate to make a sentence. Write out each sentence.

SUBJECT (topic)

1. Hagrid the giant ^ .

    —*Harry Potter and the Sorcerer's Stone*

2. Several witches in green robes ^ .

    —*Harry Potter and the Chamber of Secrets*

3. He although in the dark ^ .

    —*Harry Potter and the Goblet of Fire*

4. Voldemort's snake ^ .

    —*Harry Potter and the Deathly Hallows* (adapted)

5. A team of Healers from St. Mungo's Hospital for Magical Maladies and Injuries ^ .

    —*Harry Potter and the Half-Blood Prince*

PREDICATE (comment about topic)

a. remembered where the door into the hall was and **groped** [*felt*] his way toward it

b. are examining him as we speak

c. rose and came to rest across Voldemort's shoulders with its eyes unblinking

d. sat back down on the sofa that sagged under his weight

e. were walking onto the field with broomsticks in their hands

ACTIVITY 5: FINISHING SENTENCES

Part One Directions: Write an interesting predicate for each subject. Make your predicate several words like these examples.

EXAMPLES

> **Subject:** The spider . . .

SAMPLE PREDICATES

> **a.** The spider **crawled slowly down the web to its center.**
>
> **b.** The spider **created a beautiful web that looked like lace.**
>
> **c.** The spider **was almost invisible against the dark dead leaf.**

AUTHOR'S SENTENCE

> The spider swelled with rage, and sputtered and hissed out horrible curses.
>
> —J. R. R. Tolkien, *The Hobbit*

1. The blazing sunlight . . .
> —Matt de la Peña, *Ball Don't Lie*

2. A terrible scream . . .
> —Nancy and Benedict Freedman, *Mrs. Mike*

3. Suddenly a slim white cat . . .
> —Esther Averill, *Jenny and the Cat Club*

4. Tightly **coiled** [*curled*], the snake . . .
> —Frank Bonham, *Chief*

5. When Anjali was eight, she . . .
> —Supriya Kelkar, *Ahimsa*

Part Two Directions: Write an interesting subject for each predicate. Make your predicate several words like these examples.

EXAMPLES

Predicate: . . . found the largest snake in the place.

SAMPLE SUBJECTS

a. Our science teacher found the largest snake in the place.

b. The most experienced mountain climber found the largest snake in the place.

c. The guide in the reptile house found the largest snake in the place.

AUTHOR'S SENTENCE

Dudley quickly found the largest snake in the place.

—J. K. Rowling, *Harry Potter and the Sorcerer's Stone*

6. . . . rushed back up the stairs to wake up the family.

—Lois Duncan, *A Gift of Magic*

7. . . . had the ability to sit still.

—Madeleine L'Engle, *A Wrinkle in Time*

8. . . . had to walk right past the gates of the chocolate factory.

—Roald Dahl, *Charlie and the Chocolate Factory*

9. . . . **trudged** [*walked*] to school down a long road through the woods with his big brother and his two sisters.

—Laura Ingalls Wilder, *Farmer Boy*

10. . . . was grinning with his big teeth hanging out over his lower lip.

—Robert Lipsyte, *The Contender*

Sometimes sentences have more than one subject. Those sentences say something about more than one subject.

EXAMPLES

1. **The father and mother** talked a little about ordinary things that the boy had heard so many times. (*two subjects with same predicate*)

   —William H. Armstrong, *Sounder*

2. **Every garage, every little-used road, every patch of woods** was thoroughly investigated. (*three subjects with same predicate*)

   —Franklin W. Dixon, *The Tower Treasure*

3. The next day, **Pip, Flitter, Flap,** and **Stellaluna** went flying far from home. (*four subjects with same predicate*)

   —Janell Cannon, *Stellaluna*

Sometimes sentences have more than one predicate. Those sentences say more than one thing about the subject.

EXAMPLES

1. Ramona **scowled** and **slid down in her chair.** (*two predicates with one subject*)

   —Beverly Cleary, *Ramona and Her Father*

2. He **felt something cold on his ankles** and **looked under the tablecloth** and **saw two more of the huge worms around his ankles.** (*three predicates with one subject*)

   —Thomas Rockwell, *How to Eat Fried Worms*

3. The glow **spread, brightened,** and **burst into flames.** (*three predicates with one subject*)

   —James V. Marshall, *Walkabout*

Sometimes sentences have more than one subject AND more than one predicate. Those sentences say more than one thing about more than one subject.

EXAMPLES

1. **Frank** and **Joe Hardy clutched the grips of their motorcycles** and **stared in horror at the oncoming car**. (*two subjects and two predicates*)
    —Franklin W. Dixon, *The Tower Treasure*

2. **Alan** and **Tom** and **Joe leaned on their shovels under a tree in the apple orchard** and **watched the worms squirming on a flat rock**. (*three subjects and two predicates*)
    —Thomas Rockwell, *How to Eat Fried Worms*

3. Hastily, **he** and **I tugged on the well rope, pulled up the water tube**, and **poured the water into the bucket**. (*two subjects and three predicates*)
    —Mildred D. Taylor, *Roll of Thunder, Hear My Cry*

ACTIVITY 6: TELLING HOW MANY

Directions: These sentences have more than one subject or more than one predicate or both. Tell which. Use S+ for more than one subject, P+ for more than one predicate, S+ and P+ for more than one subject and more than one predicate.

1. He raised his leaden body and stumbled out of the room.
    —Katherine Paterson, *Bridge to Terabithia*

2. The rooster ruffled his wings, hopped over to stand beside the pig, filled his throat with air, and crowed.
    —Bill and Vera Cleaver, *Where the Lilies Bloom*

3. The gentle words, the feeling that this beast would be able to love her no matter what she said or did, **lapped** [*covered*] Meg in warmth and peace.

      —Madeleine L'Engle, *A Wrinkle in Time*

4. The four children and the Dwarf went down to the water's edge, pushed off the boat with some difficulty, and scrambled aboard.

      —C. S. Lewis, *Prince Caspian*

5. The eagle came back, seized Bilbo in his **talons** [*claws*] by the back of his coat, and **swooped** [*flew*] off.

      —J. R. R. Tolkien, *The Hobbit*

6. Squawks, screams, and croaks floated across the **humid** [*uncomfortable*] air in the forest.

      —Jean Craighead George, *The Talking Earth* (adapted)

7. Every public and private garage, every little-used road, every patch of woods was thoroughly investigated.

      —Franklin W. Dixon, *The Tower Treasure*

8. She and her father unrolled the paper across the kitchen floor and knelt with a box of crayons between them.

      —Beverly Cleary, *Ramona and Her Father*

9. The little pig gave a jump in the air, twirled, ran a few steps, stopped, looked all around, sniffed the smells of afternoon, and then set off through the orchard.

      —E. B. White, *Charlotte's Web*

10. The tall skinny Bean and dwarfish pot-bellied Bunce drove their machines like maniacs, raced the motors, and made the shovels dig at a terrific speed.

      —Roald Dahl, *Fantastic Mr. Fox*

ACTIVITY 7: ADDING SUBJECTS AND PREDICATES

Directions: These sentences have more than one subject, predicate, or both. At the word **SUBJECT**, add a subject. At the word **PREDICATE**, add a predicate. Make your addition blend well with the rest of the sentence.

1. Her eyes, skin, and **SUBJECT** were all the same color.
   —Susan Patron, *The Higher Power of Lucky* (adapted)

2. **SUBJECT** and dead rats and frogs started appearing in his locker about three months earlier.
   —Gary Paulsen, *The Time Hackers*

3. Hats and **SUBJECT** were flying in the air.
   —Jack London, *The Call of the Wild*

4. A soft, juicy hamburger spiced with relish, French fries crisp on the outside, and **SUBJECT** were Ramona's favorite payday treats.
   —Beverly Cleary, *Ramona and Her Father*

5. He reached in the back seat for the grocery bag, took out a piece of meat, bent over and unlocked the tiny door of the tiger's cage, opened it, and **PREDICATE**.
   —Kate DiCamillo, *The Tiger Rising*

6. Alfred quietly slipped out the back door and **PREDICATE**.
   —Robert Lipsyte, *The Contender*

7. The winning rodeo rider **PREDICATE**, picked himself up, picked up his hat, and waved it at the spectators.
   —Carolyn Keene, *The Secret of Shadow Ranch*

8. The cats bit and scratched and clawed each other and **PREDICATE**.
   —Wanda Gag, "Millions of Cats"

9. Judd **PREDICATE**, whipped out his wallet, and waved a twenty-dollar bill in front of my eyes.

—Phyllis Reynolds Naylor, *Shiloh*

10. Rabbits and squirrels **PREDICATE** and sometimes fall into the swimming pool.

—Wallace Stegner, *Crossing to Safety*

SUMMARY

Every sentence must have at least one subject and one predicate.

SUBJECT FACTS	
1. Subjects can be at the very beginning of the sentence.	**A wood** was on a hill above the valley. —Roald Dahl, *Fantastic Mr. Fox* (adapted)
2. Subjects can sometimes be at the end of a sentence.	On a hill above the valley was **a wood**. —Roald Dahl, *Fantastic Mr.* Fox
3. Subjects can be long.	**Being bitten by a scorpion or even a rattlesnake** is not the worst thing that can happen to you. —Louis Sachar, *Holes*
4. Subjects can be short.	**Harry** was a white dog with black spots who liked everything except getting a bath. —Gene Zion, *Harry the Dirty Dog*
5. Subjects can do just one thing.	**Vasilissa** put the skull on the end of a stick. —Post Wheeler, *Vasilissa the Beautiful*
6. Subjects can do more than one thing.	**Violet** wandered around the house, avoided Count Olaf all day, and cooked for his terrible friends every night. —Lemony Snicket, *The Bad Beginning*

7. Sentences can have just one subject.	**The velveteen rabbit** grew to like sleeping in the boy's bed. —Margery Williams, *The Velveteen Rabbit*
8. Sentences can have more than one subject.	**Cadavers** and **dead rats** and **frogs** had started appearing in his locker about three months earlier. —Gary Paulsen, *The Time Hackers*
9. Sentences must have a subject—or they won't make sense! *Without a subject, we don't know who ate lunch together.*	*(no subject)* **?** ate lunch together around the side of the building. —Louis Sachar, *There's a Boy in the Girls' Bathroom*

PREDICATE FACTS	
1. Predicates usually come after the subject.	Stars, comets, planets **flashed across the sky.** —Madeleine L'Engle, *A Wrinkle in Time*
2. Predicates sometimes come before the subject.	**On this mound among the grasses and the plants stood** Rontu. —Scott O'Dell, *Island of the Blue Dolphins*
3. Predicates can be short.	To Harry's astonishment, Dumbledore **smiled.** —J. K. Rowling, *Harry Potter and the Chamber of Secrets*
4. Predicates can be long.	Sam **caught a glimpse through an opening in the trees of the top of the green bank from which they had climbed.** —J. R. R. Tolkien, *The Fellowship of the Ring*
5. Predicates can tell just one thing.	Dad **was standing at the sink with a coffee filter in his hand.** —Laurel Snyder, *Bigger Than a Bread Box*

6. Predicates can tell more than one thing.	He **unhooked the wire, pushed the fence open, and led Shiloh to the stream for a drink after filling the pie pan with fresh water.** —Phyllis Reynolds Naylor, *Shiloh*
7. Sentences must have predicates—or they won't make sense!	Soundlessly, Nancy ? (*no predicate*) —Carolyn Keene, *The Bungalow Mystery* *Without a predicate, we don't know what Nancy did soundlessly.*

QUIZ: SUBJECTS AND PREDICATES

Directions: Tell whether the statement is true or false.

1. Sometimes complete sentences contain only a subject but no predicate.

2. Sometimes complete sentences contain only a predicate but no subject.

3. The following sentence contains a subject with exactly two parts.

   Squawks, screams, croaks, and pipings floated across the humid air in the glades.

   —Jean Craighead George, *The Talking Earth*

4. The following sentence contains a predicate with exactly two parts.

   Charles Wallace slid down from his chair and trotted over to the refrigerator.

   —Madeleine L'Engle, *A Wrinkle in Time* (adapted)

5. A sentence can have more than one subject, more than one predicate, or both.

SENTENCE-COMPOSING TOOLS

What makes the best pizza? First, you'll need a crust and a filling. Then you'll want more: maybe cheese, meat sauce, onions, peppers, pepperoni, or the works. Add-ons make it tastier, and the best.

What makes the best sentence? First, you'll need a subject and a predicate. Although necessary to have a complete sentence, subjects and predicates are not the most important sentence parts of best sentences.

The most important parts are sentence-composing tools. They add detail to your sentences. Like pizza, add-ons make sentences tastier, and the best.

The first sentence in each pair has just a subject and predicate. The second sentence has the same subject and predicate but also sentence-composing tools. Subjects are underlined once, and predicates twice. Tools are bolded.

On the Mark: Tools need commas to separate them from the rest of the sentence.

1a. The unicorn was rolling in the snow.

1b. The unicorn was rolling in the snow, **his legs up in the air, rolling and rolling, a humming of sheer pleasure coming from his throat**.
　　　　　　　—Madeleine L'Engle, *A Swiftly Tilting Planet*

2a. The herd of dinosaurs charged with surprising speed.

2b. **Honking and roaring**, the herd of dinosaurs charged with surprising speed, **their enormous bodies in a tight cluster, their infants squealing and trying to stay out from underfoot**.
　　　　　　　—Michael Crichton, *Jurassic Park*

3a. <u>He</u> <u>took a step forward</u>.

3b. Slowly rising from his hiding place, his gun still drawn, <u>he</u> <u>took a step forward</u>, **when suddenly the bush behind him seemed to explode.**

> —William P. Young, *The Shack*

4a. <u>Her eyes, skin, and hair</u> <u>were all the same color</u>.

4b. <u>Her eyes, skin, and hair</u>, **including her wispy straight eye-brows,** <u>were all the same color</u>, **a color Lucky thought of as sort of sandy or mushroomy.**

> —Susan Patron, *The Higher Power of Lucky*

5a. <u>Winston Smith</u> <u>slipped quickly through the glass doors</u>.

5b. <u>Winston Smith</u>, **his chin nuzzled into his breast in an effort to escape the horrible wind,** <u>slipped quickly through the glass doors</u>, **although not quickly enough to prevent a swirl of gritty dust entering along with him.**

> —George Orwell, *1984*

ACTIVITY 1: REVIEWING SENTENCE PARTS

Directions: Jot down the letter for the kind of sentence part:

> **S** for subject
>
> **P** for predicate
>
> **T** for tool

Note: A subject (**S**) and a predicate (**P**) are in each list. The other sentence parts are tools (**T**).

EXAMPLE *(Commas separate tools from the rest of the sentence.)*

    a. Left alone with visitors,

    b. Dimple

    c. pushed her glasses up and attempted to **rack** [*search*] her brain for something to say.

             —Sandhya Menon, *When Dimple Met Rishi*

ANSWERS

    a: T

    b: S

    c: P

Note: Sentences 1–5 contain a subject and a predicate and *one tool*.

    1a. Ms. Laverne

    1b. is looking over the new class list,

    1c. her finger moving down the row of names.

             —Jacqueline Woodson, *Harbor Me*

    2a. For a second,

    2b. I

    2c. thought she was going to cry.

             —Kelly Yang, *Front Desk*

    3a. Kim

    3b. is by the front door,

    3c. her backpack over her shoulder.

             —Jewell Parker Rhodes, *Ghost Boys* (adapted)

4a. One boy,

4b. whose name I forget,

4c. had his head down on the desk.

—Jacqueline Woodson, *Harbor Me*

5a. Across the wide blacktopped, slushy street,

5b. those two older boys

5c. caught sight of me.

—David Barclay Moore, *The Stars Beneath Our Feet*

Note: Sentences 6–10 contain a subject, a predicate, and *more than one tool*.

6a. Downstairs,

6b. my father

6c. is playing the piano,

6d. soft, sad notes floating up from the living room.

—Jacqueline Woodson, *Harbor Me*

7a. Justyce

7b. swallowed,

7c. head spinning,

7d. unable to get his **bearings** [*balance*].

—Nic Stone, *Dear Martin* (adapted)

8a. For the past two years,

8b. I

8c. attended St. Francis High School on the other side of town,

8d. away from everything and everyone I love.

> —Renée Watson, *Piecing Me Together*

9a. In these dreams,

9b. I

9c. am a famous writer,

9d. who wears **flamboyant** [*colorful*] scarves and travels all around the world,

9e. meeting fascinating people.

> —Erika L. Sanchez, *I Am Not Your Perfect Mexican Daughter*

10a. The building

10b. felt like it has exhaled,

10c. expanding a little bit without all thirty-four of us,

10d. crammed two to a desk,

10e. filling up nearly every square inch of space.

> —Aisha Saeed, *Amal Unbound*

QUESTION: What two sentence parts cannot be removed without destroying the sentence? What sentence parts can be removed without destroying the sentence, but good writers don't remove them because they add details to sentences?

ACTIVITY 2: SOLVING A SENTENCE JIGSAW PUZZLE

Directions: Connect the puzzle pieces to make a sentence. Each piece is either a subject (S), a predicate (P), or a tool (T). Every sentence has one subject and one predicate, and at least one tool. Capitalize the sentence.

On the Mark: Use commas for pause places in the sentence.

EXAMPLE

Puzzle Pieces:

a. back at the house (T)

b. inspecting his fingers and nails (T)

c. bent over his rough hands (P)

d. his mother (S)

— John Steinbeck, *The Red Pony*

Puzzle Solutions: (Others are possible.)

Back at the house, his mother bent over his rough hands, inspecting his fingers and nails. (*two commas*)

OR

Inspecting his fingers and nails, his mother, back at the house, bent over his rough hands. (*three commas*)

1. **Puzzle Pieces:**

    a. began to piece a story together (P)

    b. a secret, terrible, awful story (T)

    c. little by little (T)

    d. we (S)

    — Toni Morrison, *The Bluest Eye*

2. **Puzzle Pieces:**

   a. snapping pictures (T)

   b. taking video with their phones (T)

   c. are edging closer (P)

   d. people (S)

   > —Jewell Parker Rhodes, *Ghost Boys*

3. **Puzzle Pieces:**

   a. was seated by the cold fireplace (P)

   b. his head still bandaged (T)

   c. his broken leg resting on a wooden chair (T)

   d. he (S)

   > —Mildred D. Taylor, *Roll of Thunder, Hear My Cry*

4. **Puzzle Pieces:**

   a. the buzzards (S)

   b. in a circle around him (T)

   c. waiting for the moment of death they know so well (T)

   d. stood (P)

   > —John Steinbeck, *The Red Pony*

5. **Puzzle Pieces:**

   a. are now entering Jurassic Park (P)

   b. a world of mighty creatures long gone from the face of the earth (T)

   c. you (S)

   d. the lost world of the prehistoric past (T)

   > —Michael Crichton, *Jurassic Park*

6. Puzzle Pieces:

a. my social studies teacher (S)

b. the same guy who growled at me to sit down in the auditorium (T)

c. is Mr. Neck (P)

d. unfortunately (T)

—Laurie Halse Anderson, *Speak*

7. Puzzle Pieces:

a. sprinted back to the door and turned the key (P)

b. they (S)

c. fumbling in their panic (T)

d. wheeling around (T)

—J. K. Rowling, *Harry Potter and the Sorcerer's Stone*

8. Puzzle Pieces:

a. mimicked [*imitated*] the catbird (P)

b. its top leaves yellowed from lack of water (T)

c. in the tall locust (T)

d. a mockingbird (S)

—William H. Armstrong, *Sounder*

9. Puzzle Pieces:

a. found herself yawning (P)

b. she (S)

c. a huge yawn that stretched her diaphragm up against her heart and cracked the hinges of her jaw (T)

d. unexpectedly (T)

—Cynthia Voigt, *Dicey's Song*

10. **Puzzle Pieces:**

  a. he (S)

  b. a woman with a back bent to a curve (T)

  c. a young boy with but one leg (T)

  d. scrutinized [*examined*] the beggars at the door (P)

  e. an old man with sightless eyes praying continually (T)

  —Eric P. Kelly, *The Trumpeter of Krakow*

ACTIVITY 3: PLACING TOOLS

Directions: Put the tools into a good place within the sentence. Write out the final sentence.

On the Mark: Add commas to separate tools from the rest of the sentence.

EXAMPLE

Four dolphins were pushing the raft through the water.

—Arthur C. Clarke, *Dolphin Island*

Tool: swimming side by side

Note: Sometimes the tool can be in only one place within the sentence. Sometimes the tool can be in different places—the beginning of the sentence with one comma, the middle with two commas, or the end with one comma. Use the place you like.

Good Places:

  a. <u>Swimming side by side</u>, four dolphins were pushing the raft through the water.

b. Four dolphins, <u>swimming side by side</u>, were pushing the raft through the water.

c. Four dolphins were pushing the raft through the water, <u>swimming side by side</u>.

Note: Sentences 1–5 contain a subject and a predicate and *one tool*.

1. My mom likes to tease that I **devoured** [*ate*] the whole thing in one gulp.

> —Kelly Yang, *Front Desk*

Tool: leaving the two of them only a couple of crumbs

2. She turned toward the window.

> —Rachel Field, *Calico Bush*

Tool: pressing her cheeks to the little glass panes to cool them

3. My brothers were out of their school clothes and halfway through their homework.

> —Aisha Saeed, *Amal Unbound*

Tool: by the time I got home

4. Ashton, Tiago, and Amari pulled their seats farther back.

> —Jacqueline Woodson, *Harbor Me*

Tool: making the circle bigger and **lopsided** [*uneven*]

5. Maybe I should give my mom what she wants tonight.

> —Samira Ahmed, *Love, Hate, and Other Filters*

Tool: the dutiful daughter who is thrilled to wear gold jewelry and high heels and wants to be a doctor

----

Note: Sentences 6–10 contain a subject and a predicate and *more than one tool*.

6. I stand in the doorway.

> —Jewell Parker Rhodes, *Ghost Boys*

Tools:

> **a.** how it isn't my room anymore
>
> **b.** shocked how my room is filled with family

7. I made myself look at the floor and not stare at the top of Mr. Yao's head.

> —Kelly Yang, *Front Desk*

Tools:

> **a.** like it has been painted in egg white
>
> **b.** which was all shiny under the light

8. I leave the bedroom.

> —Jewell Parker Rhodes, *Ghost Boys*

Tools:

> **a.** searching for who spoke to me
>
> **b.** past eating, crying, praying people
>
> **c.** wandering through the apartment

9. I can hear my uncle.

> —Jacqueline Woodson, *Harbor Me*

Tools:

> **a.** neatly folding shirts and sweaters into his suitcase
>
> **b.** moving from dresser to bed and back again
>
> **c.** upstairs

10. I search for her face in the crowd of new arrivals rushing past me.
      —Ibi Zoboi, *American Street* (adapted)

   Tools:

   a. peering into every corner of this too-big place

   b. others tracking every too-bright light

   c. some with their eyes as weary as mine

ACTIVITY 4: PUTTING TOOLS INTO A PARAGRAPH

Directions: The paragraph below is about hurricanes. Put the tools in a good place within each sentence, and then write out the final paragraph.

On the Mark: Add commas to separate tools from the rest of the sentence.

1. Most hurricanes don't cause massive destruction.
   Tool: passing through an area with little or no damage, injuries, or fatalities

2. There are exceptions that set records.
   Tool: because of their devastating effects

3. The worst hurricane worldwide on record occurred in 2008.
   Tools:

   a. mainly their coastal areas on the Gulf of Mexico

   b. which struck Louisiana and Mississippi

   c. with loss of lives estimated at over 1,900 victims

   d. Hurricane Katrina in the United States

   e. and property damage over $100 billion dollars

4. Katrina's winds were not the most intense in miles per hour.

    Tool: Although Hurricane Katrina is the most devastating on record

5. That record is held by Hurricane Camille.

    Tools:

        a. the strongest ever of any hurricane making landfall

        b. with gusts as high as 210 miles per hour

        c. a storm that in 1969 raged in the North Atlantic at 190 miles per hour

6. It picked up speed in the Gulf of Mexico then headed for the coast of Mississippi, and then to the mountains of Virginia.

    Tools:

        a. and the only one of the four to cause widespread death and damage on landfall

        b. after skirting the coast of Cuba

        c. one of only four hurricanes worldwide to reach winds of 190 miles per hour

7. Estimates of the devastation include over 250 fatalities.

    TOOL: with property damage costing over 1.5 billion in 1969 dollars

TOOL FACTS	
A tool is a sentence part that adds detail to a sentence.	
1. Tools can be placed in the *beginning*, *middle*, or *end* of a sentence.	They can appear in the beginning, with a *comma after the tool*. **If a dolphin goes blind,** it can still find its way because of its powerful hearing. They can appear in the middle with a *comma before and after the tool*. Some species, **well adapted for diving to great depths**, have a barrier under the skin to keep them warm in cold water. They can appear at the end with a *comma before the tool*. Dolphins can travel thirty-five miles an hour, **using their conical shaped teeth to capture fast moving prey**.
2. A tool can be a *word*.	**WORD** **Sometimes,** dolphins are kept in captivity and trained to perform tricks.
3. A tool can be a *phrase*. A phrase is a group of words without a subject and predicate.	**PHRASE** **Called calves,** dolphin babies are usually born in the spring or summer.
4. A tool can be a *dependent clause*. A dependent clause is a sentence part containing a subject and predicate, but it is not a sentence, only a part of a sentence.	**DEPENDENT CLAUSE** **Because dolphins breathe air,** they must return to the surface to breathe.

5. Sentences can have several tools, together or apart.	**TOOLS TOGETHER** **Sometimes hunted in places like Japan, through an activity called drive hunting,** dolphins have decreased in number. **TOOLS APART** **Propelled by its powerful tail,** a dolphin can jump completely out of the water, **sometimes as high as fifteen feet in the air.**
6. Tools can be short, medium, or long.	**SHORT** Dolphins, **at four hundred pounds,** feed on fifty-three varieties of fish. **MEDIUM** In September 2018, dolphins were put on a list of endangered species, **threatened by increasing pollution and gradual destruction of the Amazon rain forest.** **LONG** Dolphins are very curious about new things, **including playing with turtles, snakes, and other fish, even playing with the oars of the boats of fishermen.**

QUIZ: SENTENCE-COMPOSING TOOLS

Directions: Jot down whether the statement is true or false.

1. Tools are complete sentences.

2. Tools can be placed at the beginning or end of a sentence but not in the middle of a sentence.

3. This sentence contains exactly three tools.

As they swung on the turn, the sled turned over, spilling half its load.

—Jack London, *The Call of the Wild* (adapted)

4. This sentence contains a subject and a predicate but no tools.

Ms. Laverne sat on the edge of the teacher's desk and folded her arms.

—Jacqueline Woodson, *Harbor Me*

5. This sentence has a subject, a predicate, and three tools. The sentence part with the fewest words is the subject:

For a long time, he just stood there, hoping the helicopter would come back, knowing that it would not.

—Robb White, *Deathwatch* (adapted)

REPAIRING BROKEN SENTENCES

FRAGMENTS

A broken sentence is called a fragment. A fragment is only a piece of sentence, not a complete sentence. Like a sentence, a fragment has a capital letter at the beginning and a period at the end, but it is a broken sentence, just a piece of a sentence. Fragments cause readers to stumble. In the activities in this section you'll learn how to get rid of them in your writing so your readers can read smoothly without stumbling.

The following examples are from J. K. Rowling's *Harry Potter and the Goblet of Fire*. In each pair below, the first is a fragment. The second gets rid of the fragment by making it part of a sentence.

EXAMPLES

1a. *Fragment*—Listening very hard.

1b. *Sentence*—Frank **inclined** [*leaned*] his good ear still closer to the door, listening very hard.

2a. *Fragment*—Fifty years before, at daybreak on a fine summer's morning.

2b. *Sentence*—Fifty years before, at daybreak on a fine summer's morning, a maid entered the drawing room to find all three Riddles dead. (adapted)

3a. *Fragment*—His back to the door, pushing the chair into place.

3b. *Sentence*—Frank caught a glimpse of a small man, his back to the door, pushing the chair into place.

4a. *Fragment*—Although it was very dark.

4b. *Sentence*—Although it was very dark, he remembered where the door into the hall was and **groped** [*felt*] his way toward it. (adapted)

5a. *Fragment*—A stranger, dark-haired and pale.

5b. *Sentence*—The only person he had seen near the house on the day of the Riddles' deaths had been a teenage boy, a stranger, dark-haired and pale.

As plates accidentally broken into fragments can be repaired, so can sentences broken into fragments.

ACTIVITY 1: SPOTTING AND GLUING FRAGMENTS

Directions: Each group has a sentence and two fragments. Tell which is the sentence, and which are the two fragments. Then glue each fragment into the sentence at the beginning or end—whichever is better.

On the Mark*:* When you glue fragments into sentences, commas are needed.

EXAMPLE

a. Holding the folder she had given him. (*fragment*)

b. He made his way through the **throng** [*crowd*]. (*sentence*)

c. Looking for his family and for Asher. (*fragment*)

GOOD ARRANGEMENTS

Holding the folder she had given him, looking for his family and for Asher, he made his way through the throng. (*Both fragments are glued at the beginning of the sentence.*)

 OR

Holding the folder she had given him, he made his way through the throng, looking for his family and for Asher. (*One fragment is glued at the beginning of the sentence, and one at the end.*)

—Lois Lowry, *The Giver*

1a. The warning that usually told them a car was coming up the road or someone was at the door.

1b. The dog started barking loudly.

1c. Ahead of them.

—Madeleine L'Engle, *A Wrinkle in Time*

2a. Looking at the back door.

2b. When Harry the Dirty Dog got to his house.

2c. He crawled through the fence and sat down.

—Gene Zion, *Harry the Dirty Dog*

3a. While the robin hopped about.

3b. He began to dig again.

3c. Driving his spade deep into the rich, black garden soil.

—Frances Hodgson Burnett, *The Secret Garden*

4a. Holding her flashlight securely.

4b. Nancy started down the lane to the house.

4c. Switching off the engine and locking the doors.

—Carolyn Keene, *The Bungalow Mystery*

5a. Making one big pile and three smaller ones.

5b. With a huge bag of yellow and red wrapped candies.

5c. Ima Dean was sitting on the floor.

—Bill and Vera Cleaver, *Where the Lilies Bloom*

ACTIVITY 2: GLUING BROKEN SENTENCES BACK TOGETHER

Directions: The paragraph below has *five* fragments that make reading bumpy. Glue each fragment to a sentence. Write out the paragraph. When you finish, you will have a paragraph with no fragments. Now, reading will be smooth, not bumpy.

On the Mark*:* When you glue a fragment to the end of a sentence, use a comma.

"The Monster in the Bedroom Window"

1. The monster roared even louder and smashed an arm through Conor's window.

2. Shattering glass and wood and brick.

3. It swung him out of his room and into the night.

4. High above his backyard.

5. Holding him up against the circle of the moon.

6. Its fingers clenching so hard against Conor's ribs he could barely breathe.

7. Conor could see raggedy teeth made of hard, knotted wood in the monster's open mouth.

8. Feeling hot breath rushing up toward him.

9. The last thing Conor remembered was the monster's mouth roaring open to eat him alive.

—Patrick Ness, *A Monster Calls*

ACTIVITY 3: SOLVING A FRAGMENT PUZZLE

Directions: The paragraph below has to be put back together. Underneath it are four broken sentences (fragments) that should be parts of the four sentences in the original paragraph. While copying the paragraph, glue each fragment to the sentence where it belongs. <u>Hint</u>: The fragments are listed in the order they occur in the original paragraph.

On the Mark: When you glue a fragment into a sentence, use a comma.

"The Death of My Dog Rags"

(1) My mother met me at the door. (2) She told me my collie, Rags, had been struck and killed by a truck. (3) I didn't cry when we buried him. (4) I cried when she told me.

—Stephen King, *11/22/63*

FRAGMENTS

Note: *The capitalized fragment begins the first sentence in the paragraph. Other fragments end a sentence in the paragraph.*

a. One day when I was nine

b. which hadn't even bothered to stop

c. although my dad told me nobody would think less of me if I did

d. partly because it was my first experience of death, but mostly because it was my responsibility to make sure Rags was safely penned up in our backyard

ACTIVITY 4: REPAIRING BROKEN SENTENCES

Directions: Make the fragment a part of a complete sentence.

EXAMPLE

<u>Fragment</u>: Because the freezing rain was dangerous.

<u>Sample Repairs</u>:

a. Because the freezing rain was dangerous, I decided to stay home and stay off the icy roads.

b. I decided to stay home and stay off the icy roads, because the freezing rain was dangerous.

Directions: Make the fragment into a sentence part <u>*at the beginning*</u> of a complete sentence.

1. <u>Fragment</u>: When the pizza was delivered to our apartment.

   <u>Sample Repair</u>: When the pizza was delivered to our apartment, we started eating it immediately.

2. <u>Fragment</u>: To figure out how to solve the math problem.

   <u>Sample Repair</u>: To figure out how to solve the math problem, you can always ask for help from your friend or your teacher.

3. <u>Fragment</u>: Early that morning when I got out of bed.

   <u>Sample Repair</u>: Early that morning when I got out of bed, I decided that taking a shower would be a good idea.

4. <u>Fragment</u>: Playing her guitar after her homework was finished.

   <u>Sample Repair</u>: Playing her guitar after her homework was finished, Louise always felt much better because of the music.

5. <u>Fragment</u>: Sometimes chasing a ball in the park.

> <u>Sample Repair</u>: Sometimes chasing a ball in the park, my dog tumbles but then continues running.

Directions: Make the fragment into a sentence part *at the end* of a complete sentence.

6. <u>Fragment</u>: A large pile of dirty laundry.

> <u>Sample Repair</u>: When my brother comes home from college, he always brings something for Mom, a large pile of dirty laundry.

7. <u>Fragment</u>: Singing the same silly song that always made us giggle.

> <u>Sample Repair</u>: My uncle would gather us kids around him, singing the same silly song that always made us giggle.

8. <u>Fragment</u>: Which they always emphasized as important.

> <u>Sample Repair</u>: My parents talked to us about being careful when crossing the street, which they always emphasized as important.

9. <u>Fragment</u>: A little puppy who often barks softly while sleeping.

> <u>Sample Repair</u>: Everyone is in love with our cute dog, a little puppy who often barks softly while sleeping.

10. <u>Fragment</u>: Talking quietly on the phone to prevent the baby from waking up.

> <u>Sample Repair</u>: The baby sitter was being very careful, talking quietly on the phone to prevent the baby from waking up.

QUIZ: BROKEN SENTENCES

Directions: Jot down whether the statement is true or false.

1. Fragments are complete sentences.

2. Fragments can be repaired.

3. Putting a capital letter at the beginning of a fragment and a period at its end repairs a fragment.

4. Fragments can always be joined to the sentence that comes before them, but never to the sentence that comes after them.

5. The paragraph below contains exactly three fragments.

> The weirdest thing happened. Her eyes began to glow. Like barbecue coals. Her fingers stretched. Turning into talons. Her jacket melted into large, leathery wings. She wasn't human. She was a shriveled **hag** [*wrinkled witch*]. With big wings and claws and a mouth full of yellow fangs. She was about to slice me to ribbons.
>
> —Rick Riordan, *The Lightning Thief*

LEARNING BY IMITATING

STARTING SENTENCE IMITATING

"Show me how." You've probably asked somebody to show you how to do something: swing a bat, fix your hair, tie a tie, ride a bike, make a grilled cheese sandwich, solve a math problem—how to do just about anything.

Imitating those who know how to do something is a good way to learn. Throughout this worktext, you'll see how authors build their sentences, imitate how they do it, and then build your sentences in a similar way.

First, look at an example of sentence imitating. Below is a model sentence followed by three sentences that imitate the way the model sentence is built. All four sentences—the model and the three imitations—mean something different and use different words, but they all have the same kinds of sentence parts. In other words, the imitations are built like the model.

EXAMPLE

Model Sentence:

> On my first day of sixth grade, I was completely and totally giddy.
>
> —Paige Rawl, *Positive: A Memoir*

Imitation Sentences:

1. On the last day before the holiday, Jane was certainly and happily excited.

2. On the last day of the year, the students were finally and thankfully finished.

3. For the opening day of her vacation, she was thoroughly and cheerfully ready.

ACTIVITY 1: FINDING THE IMITATION SENTENCE

Directions: Below each model sentence are two nonsense sentences. Which one imitates how the model sentence is built?

Note: The nonsense sentences use made-up words or they use familiar words in silly ways. Why? Well, first, it's fun! There's also another reason: using nonsense sentences will help you to focus on the structure of the sentence, not on the particular words in the sentence.

EXAMPLE

Model Sentence: This is a snail shell, round, firm, and glossy as a horse chestnut.

—Anne Morrow Lindbergh, *Gift from the Sea*

   a. There was a kran boop, squik, burd, and zilly as a boot boolock.

   b. Stamping the boomer, singing a cappy, the car kadoodled up the gazant.

Imitation Sentences: a—Sentence parts are built the same way as the model sentence.

This is a snail shell,	There was a kran boop,
round,	squik,
firm,	burd,
and glossy	and zilly
as a horse chestnut.	as a boot booglock.

1. **Model Sentence:** We ran to our bikes, my stomach churning with something like excitement.

   —John Green, *Paper Towns*

   a. Zula climbed up the kazoo, its snoleer pitching with someone like banana.

   b. When the permoota hit the babament, a turvy scooped up the flint and doop.

2. **Model Sentence:** A large woman came out from the back room, her hair in a frazzled bun.

   —Clare Vanderpool, *Moon Over Manifest*

   a. The red jelly strolled down with the green dot, its mango with a ginger tooth.

   b. Anthro, a scinty scooter with a big nostra, circled the round square.

3. **Model Sentence:** The thunder and lightning were frightening, while the rain came in gusts and torrents.

   —J. A. Swisher, "Kate Shelley," *The Palimpsest*

   a. Along the gord, with bright dirt, the grooda whirled, its hair flying off.

   b. This stoodo and poodo were contenting, when the pretzel danced in fits and turns.

4. **Model Sentence:** Until a few months ago, I was a boarding student at Yancy Academy, a private school for troubled kids.

   —Rick Riordan, *The Lightning Thief*

   a. After a few stoopoids then, he was a crimpet with Monster Mash, a fun fest for speckled droods.

   b. Its brown and yellow poondle, covered in candy, jumped the dooby bush with its putter.

5. **Model Sentence:** Anne Frank, who was thirteen when she began her diary and fifteen when she was forced to stop, wrote about her likes and dislikes.

>   —Otto H. Frank and Mirjam Pressler (editors),
>   *The Diary of Anne Frank*

  a. The bloomersnap by the butoner, covered in candles, hopped happily through the polka dot grass toward the amazing tooderman.

  b. Vander Bean, which was oily when it started its cloud and dry when it was asked to froog, jumped outside its fronts and backs.

ACTIVITY 2: CHUNKING SENTENCES

Directions: The sentence parts of the model sentence are divided into chunks (sentence parts) with a slash mark (/). Which one of the two sentences underneath the model sentence can be chunked the same way because it imitates how the model sentence is built?

EXAMPLE

  Model Sentence: I / drifted to sleep, / thinking about my cousins, / and missing them, / hoping they were missing me.

>   —Kelly Yang, *Front Desk*

  a. Painting the second coat on my bedroom walls, the same color blue, made the room feel so new and so pretty.

  b. Ashlee started to dance, jumping around the floor, and circling it, knowing her parents were watching her.

Imitation Sentences: b—Sentence parts match.

I /	Ashlee /
drifted to sleep, /	started to dance, /
thinking about my cousins, /	jumping around the floor, /
and missing them, /	and circling it, /
hoping they were missing me.	knowing her parents were watching her.

1. **Model Sentence:** It was dark / when I got up in the morning, /frosty / when I followed my breath to school.

   —Julia Alvarez, "Snow"

   a. It was a fine car, shiny with chrome and paint and sleek in shape, a red convertible designed to have a retro look from the 1950s.

   b. It was early when the bus came by from the school, late when it returned the children to their homes.

2. **Model Sentence:** She wore her coarse, straight hair, / which was slightly streaked with gray, / in a long braided rope / across the utmost top of her head.

   —Maya Angelou, *Wouldn't Take Nothing for My Journey Now*

   a. They played the grueling, championship matches, which were completely unpredictable by forecasters, with an amazing energy from the weakest players to the strongest.

   b. The arrangement, beautiful, freshly picked from the garden, smelled of a combination of lilies, sage, and magnolia to fill the room with a delightful fresh fragrance.

3. **Model Sentence:** Sometimes he cried, / tears painting lean stripes / down a grimy face, but always quietly.

> —Kristin Cashore, *Fire*

  a. Often she painted, brush making colorful shapes across a blank canvas, and never sloppily.

  b. After the party ended, they cleaned up the trash on the property and went home.

4. **Model Sentence:** Kit could see / the little wooden doll, its arms sticking stiffly / into the air, / bobbing helplessly / in the water.

> —Elizabeth George Speare, *The Witch of Blackbird Pond*

  a. Leaning out towards the ocean, Barb enjoyed the smell and the feel of a steady breeze, her hot face fanned by its softness.

  b. Adam always heard the small nonstop sound, its buzz sounding steadily in his ears, pounding monotonously in his brain.

5. **Model Sentence:** Big, rough teen-agers / moved through the crowd, / their sleeves rolled high enough / to show off / blue and red tattoos.

> —Robert Lipsyte, *The Contender*

  a. Lovely, colorful fireworks burst into the sky, their patterns bright enough to light up grey and cloudy skies.

  b. Sirens sounded throughout a crowded highway, warning that some serious event was happening nearby.

ACTIVITY 3: MATCHING

Directions: Find the imitation. Copy the imitation and its model. Then put slash marks (/) in the imitation to show the chunks (sentence parts) are the same.

MODEL SENTENCE	IMITATION SENTENCE
1. Downstairs, / my father was playing the piano, / soft, sad notes floating up / from the living room. 　　—Jacqueline Woodson, *Harbor Me*	**a.** After she was through, Sarah discovered that she hadn't listened for important facts, so she studied them with an intensity until her brain understood.
2. He stays in the air-conditioned cabin, / steering, / pressing the button, / and listening to Motown. —Jewell Parker Rhodes, *Ghost Boys* (adapted)	**b.** After you have lived as long as I have, enjoying all my life is like enjoying all delicious desserts.
3. As the boys **tumbled** [*jumped*] out of the brick schoolhouse across the field from us, / I watched from the window. 　　—Aisha Saeed, *Amal Unbound*	**c.** Nearby, the driver was changing a tire, curious, other drivers passing by on the country road.
4. When you've moved as much as I have, checking out schools is like checking out shoe polish. 　　—Kelly Yang, *Front Desk*	**d.** She goes to the nearby beach, humming, enjoying the breeze, and putting on lotion.
5. When I was seven, Amá found out I hadn't showered for five days, so she scrubbed me with a brush until my skin ached. —Erika L. Sanchez, *I Am Not Your Perfect Mexican Daughter*	**e.** When a branch appeared ahead of his horse on the path, Manuel jumped from the horse.

ACTIVITY 4: IMITATING MODEL SENTENCES

Directions: Read the model sentence and its imitation. Then write your own imitation with the same chunks (sentence parts) as the model and its imitation. Write about something you saw on TV, the Internet, or in a movie—or something you make up.

On the Mark: Put commas where they appear in the model.

1a. Model Sentence: The elephant / was dying, / in great agony, / very slowly.

> —George Orwell, "Shooting an Elephant"

1b. Imitation Sentence: The sunset / was happening, / in sudden beauty, / so colorfully.

2a. Model Sentence: In the back room / of the laboratory, / the white rats / in their cages / ran and skittered and squeaked.

> —John Steinbeck, *Cannery Row*

2b. Imitation Sentence: Near the old barn / by the railroad tracks, / the stray cat / in the wild / hunted and lived and slept.

3a. Model Sentence: She pulled out her wand, / a curved length of ivory /carved with pictures of monsters, / and pointed it / at the base of the dome.

> —Rick Riordan, *The Throne of Fire*

3b. Imitation Sentence: He put away his knife, / a straight blade of steel / stored in a holder of leather, / and kept it / in a pocket of his pants.

4a. Model Sentence: Fowler reached / across his desk, / and picked up the file, / a thin sheet of paper / neatly clipped together.

> —Clifford D. Simak, "Desertion"

4b. Imitation Sentence: Orlando searched / through his mail, / and singled out one item, / a perfumed envelope of pink / beautifully decorated overall.

5a. Model Sentence: A short, round boy of seven, / he took little interest / in troublesome things, / preferring to remain / on good terms / with everyone.

> —Mildred D. Taylor, *Roll of Thunder, Hear My Cry*

5b. Imitation Sentence: A caring, loving mother of three, / she carried great concern / for dangerous situations, / wanting to be / on constant watch / for problems.

ACTIVITY 5: MORE IMITATING

Directions: Choose one of the models and write an imitation of the entire sentence, one chunk (sentence part) at a time. See if your class can guess your model. If they can, congratulations!

MODELS

1. Henry, / the elevator operator, / is always making jokes / about me and Sheila.
   > —Judy Blume, *Tales of a Fourth Grade Nothing*

2. Before I was born, / the doctors / realized / that there was something wrong with my face.
   > —R. J. Palacio, *Wonder*

3. The penguins, / standing politely in two rows of six each, / looked curiously / at Mr. Greenbaum.
   > —Richard and Florence Atwater, *Mr. Popper's Penguins*

4. To keep ourselves / from going crazy / from boredom, / we tried / to think of word games.
   > —Barbara Kingsolver, *The Bean Trees*

5. He had / some mouthwash, / which was horrible stuff / that his mother made him gargle / when he had a cold.

> —Lynne Reid Banks, *The Return of the Indian*

QUIZ: STARTING SENTENCE IMITATING

Directions: Jot down whether the statement is true or false.

1. A good sentence imitation has the same kind of chunks as the model sentence.

2. Chunks mean the same thing as sentence parts.

3. Only some sentences can be divided into chunks.

4. Both sentences under the model sentence imitate this model sentence:

   Model Sentence: When I was in elementary school, I packed my suitcase and told my mother I was going to run away from home.

   > —Jean Craighead George, *My Side of the Mountain*

   a. Before I was on the team, I practiced my swing and told the coach I was trying to come back from the bench.

   b. Once, as a little kid, I dreamed I was big and could do everything my big brother could do so well.

5. Imitating a sentence means using your own words but only a few of the same kinds of chunks as the model sentence.

PRACTICING SENTENCE IMITATING

Sentences worth imitating are in almost everything we read. Throughout this worktext are hundreds of model sentences from all kinds of stories: popular favorites, children's literature, fantasies, sci-fi, Harry Potter novels, spy stories, horror stories, love stories, sports stories, funny stories, and on and on.

All the model sentences for imitating in *Getting Started with Elementary School Sentence Composing* include tools to build powerful sentences. After learning those tools you can become a builder of powerful sentences.

Each of the following pairs has a model sentence and an imitation of how that model sentence is built. To hear the similarity, read out loud the model and then the imitation. Notice how both are built alike.

1. From *The One and Only Ivan* by Katherine Applegate:

   Model Sentence: In the middle of the mall is a ring with benches where humans can sit on their rumps while they eat soft pretzels.

   Imitation Sentence: In the river in the Amazon is a fish with teeth where they can bite off human fingers when tourists dangle their hands.

2. From *Wonder* by R. J. Palacio:

   Model Sentence: My head on my sister's lap for a pillow, a towel wrapped around the seatbelt so I wouldn't drool all over her, I fell asleep in the backseat.

   Imitation Sentence: Her hair in a bathing cap for the dive, the goggles cleaned in the lens so she wouldn't lose any of her balance, she dove down into the pool.

3. From *Middle School* by James Patterson and Chris Tebbetts:

Model Sentence: I was at the tail end of a pretty lousy summer, which is supposed to be the best time of the year for most kids.

Imitation Sentence: He was at the exciting beginning of a brand-new friendship, which is almost always an interesting part of the relationship for both friends.

4. From *Jurassic Park* by Michael Crichton:

Model Sentence: Amid the ferns, Grant saw the head of an animal, motionless, partially hidden in the fronds, its two large dark eyes watching him coldly.

Imitation Sentence: In the distance, swimmers saw the body of a shark, obvious, easily seen in the ocean, its large dark fin nearing them slowly.

ACTIVITY 1: SPOTTING IMITATION SENTENCES

Directions: Underneath the model sentence are three sentences. Which *two* imitate the model sentence? Those two sentences are both built like the model sentence.

Note: The model sentences are from *Charlotte's Web* by E. B. White, a favorite novel of young people, the story of a friendly relationship between a pig named Wilbur and a spider named Charlotte.

EXAMPLE

Model Sentence: Although Wilbur the pig loved the spider's children, none of those spiders ever took Charlotte's place in his heart.

   a. When Tommy the lifeguard spotted the shark's appearance, all of the bathers soon obeyed his shouts for their safety.

b. Many of the spectators, gazing at the beautiful blossoms, were pleased by the low price of admission to the spectacular flower show.

c. Although Demitri the gladiator defeated the empire's contestants, one of the contestants always threatened Demitri's standing in the games.

Answer: The two sentences that imitate the model sentence are a and c. They have similar parts in similar places.

Model	Imitation	Imitation
a. Although Wilbur the pig	**a.** When Tommy the lifeguard	**a.** Although Demitri the gladiator
b. loved the spider's children,	**b.** spotted the shark's appearance,	**b.** defeated the empire's contestants,
c. none of those spiders	**c.** all of the bathers	**c.** one of the contestants
d. ever took Charlotte's place	**d.** soon obeyed his shouts	**d.** always threatened Demitri's standing
e. in his heart.	**e.** for their safety.	**e.** in the games.

1. **Model Sentence:** Wilbur planned to have a talk with Templeton, the rat that lived under his trough.

   a. The wind was stirring up the leaves on the trees, bending the lowest branches almost to the ground.

   b. No one wanted to share a meal with Harvey, the man who slept under the bridge.

   c. Harry wanted to have a dance with Shirley, the girl who lived near his house.

2. **Model Sentence:** Inside the carton, looking up at her, was a newborn pig.

   a. The last person to arrive, Dave embarrassed all his friends.

   b. Near the bush, slithering around by it, was a black snake.

   c. On the table, sitting up on a plate, was a big cake.

3. **Model Sentence:** The spider's web **glistened** [*shined*] in the light and made a pattern of loveliness, like a delicate veil.

   a. The tree's branches sagged from the snow and caused a bend in the tree, like a heavy burden.

   b. A child's smile brightened at the party and made a beautiful sign of joy, like an opening flower.

   c. Unfortunately, none of the people who had witnessed the accident could recall who was responsible.

4. **Model Sentence:** When Uncle Homer heard that the price was only six dollars, he said he would buy the pig.

   a. They changed their minds about buying the house after the storm had passed and left huge puddles of standing water.

   b. After Aunt Carmelita learned that the cost was just two dollars, she decided she could buy the flowers.

   c. Although the ringmaster knew that the tiger was only on loan, he said he could conduct the trick.

5. **Model Sentence:** While in the brook the children swam and played, Wilbur the pig amused himself in the mud along the edge of the brook, where it was warm and moist and delightfully sticky and oozy.

   a. When in the library the students studied and read, Mrs. Winston the librarian occupied herself at the desk behind the wall in a corner, where it was quiet and still and refreshingly peaceful and silent.

b. The school bus appeared long before it was expected, but the children, usually on time, were not at their designated bus stop, so the driver stayed until they came.

c. When on the field the team ran and practiced, Mr. Reynolds the coach positioned himself on the sidelines along the edge of the stands, where the team was motivated and exercising and reassuringly skillful and determined.

ACTIVITY 2: MATCHING

Directions: Match the imitation sentence with the model sentence it imitates from *Charlotte's Web* by E. B. White.

MODEL SENTENCE	IMITATION SENTENCE
1. Sometimes, on these journeys, when Wilbur the pig got tired, Fern picked him up and put him in the carriage with the doll.	**a.** Mary, the cafeteria lady, saw the crowd and came out from the school's kitchen where she was preparing lunch.
2. Lurvy, the hired man, heard the noise and came up from the asparagus patch where he was pulling weeds.	**b.** The doctor gave the little girl a shot around lunch that Monday, when she was ill at home.
3. Mrs. Arable gave the baby pig a feeding around noontime each day, when Fern was away in school.	**c.** He cried and screamed inside of the crib, yelling what an unfair decision it was and how awful it was to have a punishment.
4. Fern sat and stared out of the window, thinking what a blissful world it was and how lucky she was to have a pig.	**d.** Hearing the song about America, Mrs. Johnson stood up near the flag on the stage.
5. Carrying a bottle of milk, Fern sat down under the apple tree inside the yard.	**e.** Often, on hot days, when Tessie the toddler became uncomfortable, her mom lifted her up and dunked her in the water inside the pool.

ACTIVITY 3: UNSCRAMBLING

Directions: Unscramble the sentence parts to imitate the model sentences by authors of other stories. Start with the first sentence part listed.

On the Mark: Put commas where they appear in the model.

EXAMPLE

Model Sentence: Her heart hammering in her chest, Clary ducked behind the nearest concrete pillar and looked around it.

—Cassandra Clare, *City of Bones*

Sentence parts to unscramble to imitate the model sentence:

a. (*Start here.*) Her skin burning in the sun

b. walked to the nearest shaded area

c. and lingered in it

d. Sarah

Imitation Sentence: Her skin burning in the sun, Sarah walked to the nearest shaded area and lingered in it.

1. **Model Sentence:** Ivan the gorilla wore a snowy saddle of fur, the uniform of a silverback gorilla.

—Katherine Applegate, *The One and Only Ivan*

a. (*Start here.*) Gabriella the mascot

b. for attention

c. the signal for a big crowd cheer

d. waved a bright red flag

2. **Model Sentence:** The wolf was almost beside her, its teeth bared as it growled.

   —Jean Craighead George, *Julie of the Wolves*

   a. (*Start here.*) The sleet

   b. as they fell

   c. was nearly upon him

   d. its drops freezing

3. **Model Sentence:** When a wooden match flared, he saw James crouched like a cat, his eyes wide, sweat bubbling on his face.

   —Robert Lipsyte, *The Contender* (adapted)

   a. (*Start here.*) When a low-hanging cloud disappeared

   b. color appearing throughout the garden

   c. they saw flowers revealed like a gift

   d. their blossoms open

4. **Model Sentence:** Momma looked at Poppa's empty chair and then turned to us, her chin trembling, and told us about his accident on the highway.

   —Ingrid Law, *Savvy* (adapted)

   a. (*Start here.*) Henry listened to several opinions

   b. his mind certain

   c. and then spoke with confidence

   e. and told them about his thoughts on the problem

5. **Model Sentence:** The tyrannosaur stood near the front of the Land Cruiser, its chest moving as it breathed, the forelimbs making clawing movements in the air.

—Michael Crichton, *Jurassic Park*

a. (*Start here.*) The tractor plowed

b. the driver leading farmworkers through the field

c. toward the end of the cornfield

d. its shovels digging as it moved

ACTIVITY 4: IMITATING SENTENCES

Directions: The following model sentences are adapted from *The Incredible Journey* by Sheila Burnford, a story of three pets—two dogs and one cat—traveling over three hundred miles to find their loving owners. Each model has two imitation sentences. Study the model and the two imitations, and then write your own imitation, one sentence part at a time. Write about something you saw on TV, the Internet, or in a movie—or something you make up.

Model One—This was a deer mouse, a little creature with big eyes and long hind legs like a miniature kangaroo.

Model	Imitation	Imitation
a. This was a deer mouse,	**a.** This is an amazing gadget,	**a.** He was an Olympic star,
b. a little creature	**b.** a small piece	**b.** a talented swimmer
c. with big eyes	**c.** of music technology	**c.** with iron determination
d. and long hind legs	**d.** and unlimited song selections	**d.** and very long arms
e. like a miniature kangaroo.	**e.** like a forever band.	**e.** like a motorized paddle.

Model Two—The old dog ate, crunching the bones **ravenously** [*hungrily*] with his poor teeth.

Model	Imitation	Imitation
a. The old dog ate,	**a.** The fierce storm raged,	**a.** The downhill skier raced,
b. crunching the bones ravenously	**b.** whipping the branches constantly	**b.** beating his record easily
c. with his poor teeth.	**c.** with its strong force.	**c.** in a surprising comeback.

Model Three—The young dog slept poorly, his muscles twitching, constantly lifting his head and growling softly.

Model	Imitation	Imitation
a. The young dog	**a.** The new team	**a.** The traveling octopus
b. slept poorly,	**b.** played awkwardly,	**b.** swam carefully,
c. his muscles twitching,	**c.** their skill declining,	**c.** its tentacles reaching,
d. constantly lifting his head	**d.** always doubting their ability	**d.** carefully inspecting some food
e. and growling softly.	**e.** and watching timidly.	**e.** and eating slowly.

Model Four—Head down, tail flying, the young dog chased the rabbit, swerving and turning in **pursuit** [*chase*].

Model	Imitation	Imitation
a. Head down,	**a.** Top down,	**a.** Jaws open,
b. tail flying,	**b.** chrome shining,	**b.** body diving,
c. the young dog	**c.** the red convertible	**c.** the hungry shark
d. chased the rabbit,	**d.** cruised the neighborhood,	**d.** stalked its victim,
e. swerving	**e.** shimmering	**e.** gliding
f. and turning	**f.** and flashing	**f.** and swimming
g. in pursuit.	**g.** in sunlight.	**g.** with purpose.

Model Five—Satisfied at last, the cat stretched **superbly** [*impressively*], his front paws like a library lion statue, then jumped onto Helvi's lap, curled himself around, and purred loudly.

Model	Imitation	Imitation
a. Satisfied at last,	**a.** Completed over years,	**a.** Educated in stunts,
b. the cat stretched superbly,	**b.** the tower rose impressively,	**b.** magician Houdini stood confidently,
c. his front paws	**c.** its iron pillars	**c.** his bound arms
d. like a library lion statue,	**d.** like a strong permanent foundation,	**d.** like an inescapable straitjacket,
e. then jumped	**e.** then reached	**e.** then jumped
f. onto Helvi's lap,	**f.** into Paris' skyline,	**f.** into a water tank,
g. curled himself around,	**g.** made itself famous,	**g.** held his breath,
h. and purred loudly.	**h.** and stood majestically.	**h.** and escaped miraculously.

ACTIVITY 5: IMITATING PARAGRAPHS

Directions: Which of the two paragraphs under the model paragraph imitates how the model's sentences are built?

___ **EXAMPLE**
- - - - - - - - - - - -

___ **MODEL**
- - - - - - - - - -

(1) The body is marvelous at letting us know how much water we need. (2) Diet, exercise, and the environment all play a role. (3) If you eat lots of foods naturally rich in water, such as vegetables, fruits, and whole grains, you may not need to drink much water. (4) If you don't eat salty foods, you need less drinking water.

—Larry Scheckel, *Ask Your Science Teacher*

Paragraph A

(1) People can control their thoughts, and can think just about anything. (2) Our thoughts are made up of our experiences. (3) You can think happy thoughts so that you don't have to deal with lots of unpleasant thoughts. (4) People who think mainly pleasant thoughts don't want to control their thoughts because they enjoy those thoughts and don't want to change them.

Paragraph B

(1) The mind is amazing at helping us think whatever we wish. (2) People, places, and situations all contribute to thought. (3) If you think lots of thoughts very optimistic in content, such as memories, dreams, and pleasant wishes, you may not need to control your thoughts. (4) If you don't think unpleasant thoughts, you need less thought control.

Answer: Paragraph B has sentences built like those in the model. Read each sentence from the left column, then each sentence from the right column to see how they are built alike.

Model Paragraph	Imitation Paragraph
1. The body is marvelous at letting us know how much water we need.	**1.** The mind is amazing at helping us think whatever we wish.
2. Diet, exercise, and the environment all play a role.	**2.** People, places, and situations all contribute to thought.
3. If you eat lots of foods naturally rich in water, such as vegetables, fruits, and whole grains, you may not need to drink much water.	**3.** If you think lots of thoughts very optimistic in content, such as memories, dreams, and pleasant wishes, you may not need to control your thoughts.
4. If you don't eat salty foods, you need less drinking water.	**4.** If you don't think unpleasant thoughts, you need less thought control.

MODEL ONE

(1) I found a faded photograph of my dog Skip not long ago, his long **snout** [*nose*] sniffing at something in the air, his tail straight and pointing. (2) Looking at that faded photograph taken more than forty years before, I still miss him.

—Willie Morris, *My Dog Skip* (adapted)

Paragraph A

(1) I knew my punishment was going to cost me some of my allowance and also some of my freedom. (2) To be honest, I should never have told the lie that led to my scolding, a fib about why I hadn't told them the truth about school.

Paragraph B

(1) My grandmother assembled an album of our extended family many years ago, its yellowing photos smelling of moth balls from the attic, her choices varied and interesting. (2) Glancing through that family album assembled more than seventy years ago, I deeply loved her.

MODEL TWO

(1) His face sad, he dropped back helplessly, tears running down his cheeks. (2) His mother leaned over him, her arms round him, murmuring soothingly as if he were a baby. (3) In a few moments he began to relax, and breathe more easily.

—Susan Cooper, The Grey King

Paragraph A

(1) She was a new student in the class, uncertain and nervous. (2) Her teacher took her around the room to introduce her to all the other students. (3) Later that day, she started to realize how pleasant this situation might be for her in a new school.

Paragraph B

(1) His body tense, he sank in uncontrollably, panic racing through his brain. (2) His friend stayed beside him, his voice near him, coaching quietly as if he were a beginner. (3) After a little while he started to concentrate, and think more clearly.

MODEL THREE

(1) The ship plowed through wave after wave, trembling, careening on its side, yet somehow managing to stay afloat. (2) Zigzagging through the sky, the sharp cracks of lightning, never **diminishing** [*lessening*], resounded on the water. (3) From the passageway, Alec saw one of the crew make his way along the deck, desperately fighting to hold on to the rail. (4) The ship rolled sideways and a huge wave swept over the boat. (5) When it passed, the sailor was gone.

—Walter Farley, The Black Stallion

Paragraph A

(1) The runner raced through mile after mile, counting on his conditioning, but sometimes wanting to stop going. (2) Pounding over the road, the constant pain in his feet, always throbbing, increased over the miles. (3) Along his side, Frank saw one of the runners slow his pace near the hill, probably wanting to slow down on the incline. (4) That runner wobbled noticeably, and a sympathetic crowd moved toward the contestant. (5) As they cheered, the runner was revived.

Paragraph B

(1) The boomerang was invented by the Australian aborigines, who used it for sport and play. (2) A boomerang is thrown by one person to whom it will return, coming back in the same arc. (3) The oldest boomerang was discovered in Poland made of a mammoth's tusk. (4) This ancient boomerang did not return to the person who threw it, so historians think it was used for hunting. (5) The fascination of something that can be thrown and return to the thrower makes the boomerang a popular toy.

MODEL FOUR

(1) During the bitterly cold days of winter, the thirteen-year-old had gotten into the habit of counting the blocks until she was safe at home, safe from the freezing cold wind, safe from the nasty comments made by girls who had cut school and were always hanging out in front of the local drugstore, safe from the gang of boys who had all but quit school and who hung out in the broken-down playground in front of her building. (2) They all seemed to have something mean to say about her.

—Traci L. Jones, *Standing Against the Wind*

Paragraph A

(1) During the long boring hours of work, the young man had begun the practice of imagining the future when he was beyond this job, beyond the mindless same tasks, beyond the endless requests made by bosses who had made money and were only looking around for cheap labor, beyond the type of people who had never forecast a future and who looked ahead in their own minds to more of the same horrible kind of work. (2) No one hoped to have something better to imagine for themselves.

Paragraph B

(1) From 1892 to 1924 more than twelve million immigrants sailed past the Statue of Liberty in New York harbor to start their lives over in America. (2) Coming from all over Europe, they landed at Ellis Island, hoping for a better life in America than the one they left behind in Europe, wanting a chance at success in a new and less threatening place, seeking to make a better future for their children.

MODEL FIVE

(1) Then, beyond the noise of his own sobs, Matt heard a voice calling, clear and strong and real, a child's voice. (2) Matt ran to the window. (3) Then a shadow crossed the opening, and Matt **recoiled** [*jumped*] so quickly that he fell over and landed on the floor. (4) The door handle rattled as Matt squatted on the floor, his heart pounding. (5) Someone put his face against the window, cupping his hands to see through the gloom. (6) Matt froze.

—Nancy Farmer, *The House of the Scorpion*

Paragraph A

(1) Next, at the sound of the familiar cheerful voice, Sharon recognized the visitor approaching, quick and joyful and mischievous, her best friend. (2) Sharon went to the door. (3) Then a smile lit her friend's face, and she ran so eagerly that she tripped but got to her feet. (4) The front door opened as her friend bounced into the room, her spirits leaping. (5) Sharon shook her head at the sight, covering her mouth to keep from shouting. (6) They laughed.

Paragraph B

(1) When you are camping or hiking in bear country, you need to make noise to let them know you are in the area. (2) A bear may be attracted to food that you have brought. (3) For that reason, hang your food from a rope between two trees. (4) A hungry bear will not bother you if you are careful. (5) It is a good idea to burn any garbage and leftover food, and not go anywhere alone where bears might be in the woods. (6) Be careful, and stay safe.

QUIZ: PRACTICING SENTENCE IMITATING

Directions: Jot down whether the statement is true or false.

1. Imitating is one way to learn something.

2. Imitating sentences means using your own words but the author's sentence structure.

3. Imitating sentences by authors helps you to build stronger sentences.

4. A good sentence imitation has many of the same words as the ones in the model sentence.

5. Only two sentences underneath the model sentence are built like the model:

> **Model Sentence:** On impulse, he went in, bought a bag of gumdrops, and went on up the street, his mouth full of candy.
>
> —Hal Borland, *When the Legends Die*

(1) After school, she went home, ate a snack of chips, and went on into her room, her lips covered with salt.

(2) At night, Albert looked out, saw a crowd of neighbors, and went on out the door, his thoughts filling with questions.

(3) For hours, cars moved slowly, rounded the scene of the accident, and drove on around the scene, their drivers steering with caution.

THE SENTENCE-COMPOSING TOOLS

USING SENTENCE-COMPOSING TOOLS

Sentence-composing tools can occur at the beginning of a sentence (openers), the middle of a sentence (splits), the end of a sentence (closers).

In the following activity, the left column shows basic sentences with just a subject and a predicate. The right column shows sentence-composing tools that have been removed from those basic sentences. In this activity, you'll put those tools back in at the caret mark (^) to make a better sentence.

ACTIVITY 1: ADDING TOOLS

Directions: At the caret (^), insert the tool into the sentence. Write out the sentence. Notice that the left column has a complete sentence with a subject and a predicate. It can stand alone. The right column, though, has just sentence parts that must be a part of a complete sentence.

Sentence	Tool
1. ^, a great chapter in American life came to a close. (*opener*) —Bruce Catton, "The American Story"	When Grant and Lee met in a modest house at Appomattox, Virginia, on April 9, 1865, for the surrender of Lee's army
2. My soaked grandmother, ^ , burst into my mother's room. (*split*) —John Irving, *A Prayer for Owen Meany*	dripping wet, her usually flowing nightgown plastered to her **gaunt** [*thin*], hunched body
3. Crows circled the sky before landing in the snow-covered fields, ^ . (*closer*) —Diane Ackerman, *The Zookeeper's Wife*	on one of those warm January mornings when just breathing feels like inhaling cotton

4. ^ , Violet closed her eyes and began to climb with her hands grasping the rope. (*opener*) —Lemony Snicket, *A Series of Unfortunate Events*	Her feet touching the side of the stone tower
5. Sophie, ^ , peeped out of the cave. (*split*) —Roald Dahl, *The BFG*	sitting on the Big Friendly Giant's hand
6. The elephant was tearing up bunches of grass, ^ . (*closer*) —George Orwell, "Shooting an Elephant"	beating them against his knees to clean them and stuffing them into his mouth

ACTIVITY 2: COMBINING

Directions: Combine two sentences into one sentence. Make the underlined part a tool to insert at the caret (^) in the first sentence. Write out the sentence.

EXAMPLE

Opener:

^ , I wore a pirate patch on my good eye to make the muscles in the bad one get stronger. This happened <u>when I was little</u>.

Combined: <u>When I was little</u>, I wore a pirate patch on my good eye to make the muscles in the bad one get stronger.

—Meg Medina, *Merci Suárez Changes Gears*

---

1. ^ , the soldiers' uniforms glowed a deep purple **hue** [*color*]. The glow was happening <u>in the gloom before the break of the day</u>.

—Stephen Crane, *The Red Badge of Courage*

2. ^ , I lay panting on the edge of the pool and began to feel my wrist. I lay there with <u>pain shooting up my entire arm</u>.

—Theodore Taylor, *The Cay*

3. ^, Eliza stopped bleeding. It stopped <u>finally, near dawn</u>.

—Isabel Allende, *Daughter of Fortune*

4. ^, Mother Smith was a thin **feisty** [*lively*] little woman who had been quite a beauty when she was younger. She was <u>unlike her son Doc, who was easygoing</u>.

—Fannie Flagg, *Standing in the Rainbow*

5. ^ , Tim was knocked flat on the seat, blinking in the darkness, his mouth warm with blood. Tim's injury happened <u>after the tyrannosaur's head crashed against the hood of the Land Cruiser and shattered the windshield</u>.

—Michael Crichton, *Jurassic Park*

EXAMPLE

Split:

Her big brown eyes, ^ , were warmer, softer. Her eyes were <u>like berries that had ripened.</u>

Combined: Her big brown eyes, <u>like berries that had ripened</u>, were warmer, softer.

—Mary Lavin, "One Summer"

---

6. The train, ^ , slowed to a halt. It slowed <u>with a creak</u>.

—Truman Capote, "A Ride Through Spain"

7. Pressure against the body, ^ , causes a **tarantula** [*spider*] to move off slowly for a short distance. The pressure may be made <u>by a finger or the end of a pencil</u>.

    —Alexander Petrunkevitch, "The Spider and the Wasp"

8. The tent, ^ , glowed warmly in the midst of the plain. The tent was **illumined** [*lighted*] <u>by a candle</u>.

    —Jack London, *The Call of the Wild*

9. This room, ^ , sat in the rear of a house unfamiliar to Candace. The room was <u>small and cramped</u>.

    —Varian Johnson, *The Parker Inheritance*

10. The flame, ^ , **enveloped** [*covered*] in a small twig, reached up to a branch, which exploded with a sharp crack. The flame had been <u>invisible at first in that bright sunlight</u>.

    —William Golding, *Lord of the Flies* (adapted)

EXAMPLE

Closer:
Street artists and caricaturists were in full cry as we passed them, ^ .
They were **raucous** [*loud*] <u>as crows.</u>

Combined: Street artists and caricaturists were in full cry as we passed them, <u>raucous as crows</u>.

   —Pat Conroy, *My Losing Season*

11. The drops of blood from the injured soldier fell very slowly, ^ . The drops fell <u>as they fall from an icicle after the sun has gone</u>.

    —Ernest Hemingway, *A Farewell to Arms*

12. Boo drifted to a corner of the room where he stood with his chin up. He was **peering** [*looking*] <u>from a distance at Jem</u>.

    —Harper Lee, *To Kill a Mockingbird*

13. Lisey awoke in the deepest ditch of the night, ^ . That time of night is <u>when the moon is down</u>.

—Stephen King, *Lisey's Story*

14. Halfway there he heard the sound he dreaded, ^ . The sound was <u>the hollow, **rasping** [*awful*] cough of a horse</u>.

—John Steinbeck, *The Red Pony*

15. He was twenty at the time, ^ . He was <u>a tall young man in ill-fitting clothes, his hair very black and cut too short, his face a shade too thin, with dark whiskers</u>.

—Anne Tyler, *The Amateur Marriage*

ACTIVITY 3: MATCHING

The fifteen sentences in the following activities are adapted from *A Walk in Wolf Wood* by Mary Stewart, a fantasy in which two children in the woods meet a mysterious man who becomes a werewolf.

Directions for Tools as Openers: Find the tool that opens the sentence. Write out the sentence putting the tool at the caret (^).

On the Mark: Use one comma after the tool to separate it from the rest of the sentence.

TOOLS AS OPENERS	SENTENCE
1. Quickly but secretly	**a.** ^ , John looked down at her.
2. When he spoke	**b.** ^ , the children crept through the waist-high fern and bramble.
3. With a shrill, cross little song	**c.** ^ , Margaret's brother had to work hard to keep his voice cheerful.

| 4. As soon as night fell | d. ^ , he would go out into the forest as a werewolf to kill and eat his fill. |
| 5. Balancing on a tree trunk | e. ^ , a wren flew down onto the ferns nearby. |

Directions for Tools as Splits: Find the tool that splits the sentence. Write out the sentence, putting the tool at the caret (^).

On the Mark: Use one comma before the tool and one comma after it to separate it from the rest of the sentence.

TOOLS AS SPLITS	SENTENCE
6. a monster of the night	a. Moths, ^ , floated up from the disturbed leaves like feathers from a shaken torn pillow.
7. waking for the night	b. The Duke, ^ , caught his spur in the stirrup and was dragged before I could stop his horse.
8. clutching one another's hands	c. The werewolf, ^ , could see in darkness as well as any cat or owl.
9. although dusty and unused	d. The children, ^ , backed away from the werewolf's long, terrible howl.
10. in falling from his horse	e. The secret room, ^ , showed no signs of decay.

Directions for Tools as Closers: Find the tool that closes the sentence. Write out the sentence putting the tool at the caret (^).

On the Mark: Use one comma before the tool to separate it from the rest of the sentence.

TOOLS AS CLOSERS	SENTENCE
11. leaving the open door as they had found it	a. The werewolf's paws approached the children's door, ^ .
12. in the middle of the dark and deserted woods	b. An enormous wolf stood in the cottage doorway, ^ .
13. with a scratching and clicking of claws on wood	c. The children stood very still, ^ .
14. its yellow eyes fixed on the children, its jaws open and long tongue out	d. Margaret and John crept out of the doorway, ^ .
15. rooted in terror	e. Their parents had driven away and left them alone, ^ .

ACTIVITY 4: ADDING TOOLS

Directions: Underneath each basic sentence are tools from the original sentence. Add the tools where they make the most sense—*opener, split,* or *closer.*

On the Mark: If a tool needs a pause before or after it, or both, use a comma.

EXAMPLE

Basic Sentence: Harry got to his feet and set off again as fast as he could without making too much noise.

Tools:

    a. very slowly and very carefully

    b. hurrying through the darkness back toward Hogwarts

Original Sentence: <u>Very slowly and very carefully,</u> Harry got to his feet and set off again as fast as he could without making too much noise, <u>hurrying through the darkness back toward Hogwarts.</u> (*opener* and *closer*)

        —J. K. Rowling, *Harry Potter and the Goblet of Fire*

---

1. I used to think that everyone knew something I didn't.

   a. until I was a young adult

   b. from as far back as I can remember

           —Mike Dooley, *Infinite Possibilities*

2. He struck most of his friends as an **eccentric** [*original*].

   a. a harmless one

   b. an **unruly** [*wild*] guy with odd habits

           —Douglas Adams, *A Hitchhiker's Guide to the Galaxy*

3. She could see herself in the side mirror.

   a. her sunglasses reflecting the prairie grass

   b. her hair rippling

           —Dan Chaon, *Await Your Reply* (adapted)

4. Winston Smith slipped quickly through the glass doors.

   a. though not quickly enough to prevent dust entering along with him

   b. his chin **nuzzled** [*lowered*] into his breast in an effort to escape the wind

           —George Orwell, *1984*

5. The Indians ran to greet them.

   a. bringing them food, water, gifts

   b. when Columbus and his sailors came ashore

   > —Howard Zinn, *A People's History of the United States*

6. The desert around our house seemed to have no reason for existence.

   a. dotted with sticker bushes, tumbleweed, and coiled rattlesnakes

   b. other than providing a place for people to dump things

   > —Andre Agassi, *Open: An Autobiography*

7. He felt the young man's joy at seeing his brother alive.

   a. and buried in a forgotten part of the forest

   b. the brother he had thought dead

   > —Madeleine L'Engle, *A Swiftly Tilting Planet*

8. He remembered a chipmunk.

   a. and sat in his hand

   b. a pet that came when he called

   c. that he had as a small boy

   > —Hal Borland, *When the Legends Die*

9. I continued to wait.

   a. the other clinging to the raft

   b. as the rain crashed down on the raft

   c. one hand gripping the rain catcher

   > —Yann Martel, *Life of Pi* (adapted)

10. He **scrutinized** [*examined*] the beggars at the door.

    a. and many other homeless people

b. an old man with sightless eyes praying continually

c. a young boy with but one leg

—Yann Martel, *Life of Pi* (adapted)

ACTIVITY 5: REVIEWING OPENERS, SPLITS, CLOSERS

Directions: Using these abbreviations, tell the place of the tool in the sentence.

> **O**—opener
> **S**—split
> **C**—closer

1. Miss Edmunds fiddled a minute with her guitar, talking as she tightened the strings.
   —Katherine Paterson, *Bridge to Terabithia*

2. Because he was so small, Stuart the little mouse was often hard to find around the house.
   —E. B. White, *Stuart Little*

3. Chantilly, the neighbor girl's cat, was sunning on the porch steps.
   —Patricia C. McKissack, *A Million Fish, More or Less*

4. Mr. Anderson grasped the arms of the chair, his knuckles chalk white.
   —Mildred D. Taylor, *Song of the Trees*

5. The first floor, because it was closest to the garbage in the empty lot, was where the rats lived.
   —Walter Dean Myers, *Motown and Didi*

6. While Romey was gone, I started peeling, slicing, and frying the onions.
   —Bill and Vera Cleaver, *Where the Lilies Bloom*

7. Looking up at the sky, Sara began to kick her foot back and forth in the deep grass.

    —Betsy Byars, *The Summer of the Swans*

8. He was Tom Black Bull, a man who had come to the end of his long hunt.

    —Hal Borland, *When the Legends Die*

9. The biggest reader of the three children, Klaus was the most likely to know vocabulary words and foreign phrases.

    —Lemony Snicket, *The Bad Beginning*

10. Dr. John Lilly, the first scientist to attempt communication with dolphins, had suggested ways in which they might co-operate with man.

    —Arthur C. Clarke, *Dolphin Island*

11. After I figured out how punctuation worked, I read all my old Progress Reports from the beginning.

    —Daniel Keyes, *Flowers for Algernon*

12. Mrs. Rachel, before she closed the door, took mental note of everything that was on that table.

    —L. M. Montgomery, *Anne of Green Gables*

13. He turned on the television, piping through the house the sound of news reports that were happening so far from here that they barely seemed real.

    —Kekla Magoon, *The Season of Styx Malone*

14. Her dear mamma, who had died when she was born, was French.

    —Frances Hodgson Burnett, *A Little Princess*

15. He snapped awake and scrambled clumsily to his feet, his muscles sore and stiff from lying on the floor.

—William P. Young, *The Shack*

ACTIVITY 6: USING TOOLS IN YOUR SENTENCES

Directions: After reading the sample sentences, write *one* of your own sentences with a similar tool. Write about something you remember from your own life or something you make up. *Important*: Your tool must be a sentence part, not a complete sentence.

---

1. Some tools start with one of these words: *although, before, because, when, while,* or *until.* Write a sentence with a tool starting with *although, before, because, when, while,* or *until.* Decide the best place for your tool—opener, split, or closer.

SAMPLE SENTENCES

a. *Opener*—**When** <u>Harry the Dirty Dog got to his house</u>, he crawled through the fence and sat down and looked at the back door.

—Gene Zion, *Harry the Dirty Dog* (adapted)

b. *Split*—Saturday morning, **although** <u>it was brilliantly sunny</u>, was overcoat weather again.

—J. D. Salinger, *Franny and Zooey* (adapted)

c. *Closer*—He beat the creature off with his hands, **until** <u>he remembered his sword and drew it out</u>.

—J. R. R. Tolkien, *The Hobbit*

---

2. Some tools start with one of these words: *her, his,* or *its.* Write a sentence with a tool starting with *her, his,* or *its.* Decide the best place for your tool—opener, split, or closer.

SAMPLE SENTENCES

a. *Opener*—**His** hand trembling, Billy laid the peanut-butter-and-fried-worm sandwich down on the table.

—Thomas Rockwell, *How to Eat Fried Worms*

b. *Split*—A teenager in a black tank top, **her** greenish tattoo flowing across her broad back, **hoisted** [*lifted*] a toddler onto her shoulder.

—Barbara Kingsolver, *Animal Dreams*

c. *Closer*—Harry twisted his body around and saw a grindylow with its pointed fangs **bared** [*showing*], **its** long fingers holding tightly around Harry's leg.

—J. K. Rowling, *Harry Potter and the Goblet of Fire* (adapted)

3. Some tools start with one of these words: *a* or *the.* Write a sentence with a tool starting with *a* or *the.* Decide the best place for your tool—opener, split, or closer.

SAMPLE SENTENCES

a. *Opener*—**A** small man, he wore a cotton shirt and a long, blood-stained smock.

—Christopher Paolini, *Eragon*

b. *Split*—Jack, **the** meanest boy I have ever known in my life, called me bad names.

—Jean Stafford, *Bad Characters*

c. *Closer*—Inside the cage next to the gas station, unbelievably, there was a tiger, <u>**a** real-life, very large tiger pacing back and forth</u>.

—Kate DiCamillo, *The Tiger Rising*

4. Some tools start with a word that ends with these three letters: *ing*. Write a sentence starting with a tool ending with *ing*. Decide the best place for your tool—opener, split, or closer.

SAMPLE SENTENCES

a. *Opener*—<u>**Glaring** at us sternly</u>, he motioned with a bony finger for us to follow him.

—R. L. Stine, *Ghost Beach*

b. *Split*—The poor fellow, <u>**looking** thin and starved</u>, was sitting there trying to eat a bowl full of mashed-up green caterpillars.

—Roald Dahl, *Charlie and the Chocolate Factory*

c. *Closer*—The stallion tried to escape, <u>**charging** against the board of his stall again and again</u>.

—Marguerite Henry, *Misty of Chincoteague*

QUIZ: USING SENTENCE-COMPOSING TOOLS

Directions: Jot down whether the statement is true or false.

1. The sentence below has a closer.

One of the ancient pyramids is composed of two million blocks of stone, weighing more than two tons for each stone.

—Conn and Hal Iggulden, *The Dangerous Book for Boys*

2. The sentence below has an opener.

> The winner of hopscotch is the first player to complete one course of hopping up and back for every numbered square.

> —Andrea J. Buchanan and Miriam Peskowitz,
> *The Daring Book for Girls*

3. The sentence below has a split.

> The missing part of my leg, the part that was **amputated** [*cut off*], burned with a phantom pain.

> —Wendelin Van Draanen, *The Running Dream* (adapted)

4. The sentence below has no tools.

> Carolina nodded, trying to smile.

> —Emma Otheguy, *Silver Meadows Summer*

5. The sentence below has an opener and two closers.

> When Mama gets to especially tangled places in my hair, I try my hardest not to cry, sucking in my breath, pressing my hands together.

> —Natasha Anastasia Tarpley, *I Love My Hair!* (adapted)

THE TOOLBOX

To get the job done right, use the right tools in the right places. You've learned *the opener, the split, the closer*. Now get ready to use them. When you finish, admire your work, done right with the right tools in the right places, and take a bow!

ACTIVITY 1: PLACING ONE TOOL

Directions: Following are sentences about famous people. Add **one** of the listed tools in a good place in the sentence. Copy the sentence, underline the tool, and name its position.

On the Mark: Use a comma to separate the tool from the rest of the sentence.

1. Babe Ruth is the greatest baseball player of all time.

    a. because he achieved so many records

    b. several of his records still standing to this day

    c. the holder of many records like runs batted in

    d. achieving his greatest fame as a slugging outfielder for the New York Yankees.

2. Cleopatra in ancient Egypt was the most powerful woman in the world.

    a. when she allied with some of the most powerful forces of her time

    b. her story told in many movies, stories, and operas

    c. the most powerful female pharaoh in Egyptian history

    d. taking the throne as a teenager

3. Mahatma Gandhi led the India movement toward independence from British rule.

   a. since he was successful at using nonviolent civil disobedience

   b. his achievement resulting in self-rule for India

   c. a model for Dr. Martin Luther King Jr. in King's civil rights movement

   d. inspiring worldwide attempts for freedom through nonviolent protests

4. John Kennedy was the thirty-fifth president of the United States.

   a. although he was the first Catholic elected to the presidency

   b. his heroism revealed during World War II when he saved the lives of his crew

   c. a member of a large and politically active family

   d. assassinated in a motorcade in Dallas, Texas, in 1963 with his wife beside him

5. Abraham Lincoln served as the sixteenth president of the United States.

   a. after he had grown up on the prairie and was self-taught

   b. his popularity with historians and the public among the greatest

   c. the author of the Emancipation Proclamation

   d. composing the Gettysburg Address on a train on his way to the battlefield

ACTIVITY 2: PLACING TWO TOOLS

Directions: Add a mix of **two** of the listed tools in good places in the sentence. Copy the sentence, underline the tools, and name their positions.

On the Mark: Use commas to separate tools from the rest of the sentence.

6. American astronaut Neil Armstrong was the first person to walk on the moon.

   a. when the Apollo 11 Lunar Module landed

   b. his moon exploration lasting two and a half hours

   c. a naval test pilot and university professor

   d. stating "That's one small step for man, one giant leap for mankind"

7. Alexander Hamilton was one of America's founding fathers.

   a. because he established the American system of money

   b. his life the subject of the Broadway hit musical *Hamilton*

   c. an immigrant to New York City from his native British West Indies

   d. dying in 1804 from a pistol duel with political enemy Aaron Burr

8. Walt Disney is famous for his creation of animated movies.

   a. although he died before the opening of Walt Disney World in Florida

   b. his reputation as an innovator in film animation never matched

   c. the creator of the character Mickey Mouse

   d. holding a record of twenty-two Academy Awards for his movies

9. Aretha Franklin was considered the queen of soul.

    a. because she sang deeply emotional and rhythmic songs

    b. her efforts in civil rights and women's rights successful

    c. the first female to be inducted into the Rock and Roll Hall of Fame

    d. becoming the most charted female singer on Billboard's top hit songs lists

10. Anne Frank wrote her diary.

    a. when she was in hiding to escape the Nazis during the holocaust

    b. her adolescent thoughts and longings described powerfully

    c. a much discussed young victim of the holocaust

    d. inspiring several plays and films about her young life

ACTIVITY 3: CREATING ONE TOOL

Directions: Below are sentences about famous persons. Choose any **five** sentences to create then insert **one tool** into each sentence. Underline the tool, and name its position in parentheses: *opener, split, closer.* Before creating your tool, first learn more about the person online so your tool will be informative and interesting.

1. Harry Houdini was a famous magician and escape artist.

2. Stephen King has terrified millions of readers and viewers.

3. Serena Williams became an award-winning tennis player.

4. Cassius Clay was also known as Muhammad Ali.

5. Helen Keller did not let her blindness limit her life.

6. Michael Jordan was the greatest basketball player of all time.

7. John Lennon was a rock singer and peace activist.

8. Thomas Edison invented the light bulb and changed the world.

9. Mark Zuckerberg cofounded Facebook.

10. George Washington was the first president of the United States.

ACTIVITY 4: CREATING A MIX OF TWO TOOLS

Directions: Below are sentences about famous places or things. Choose any **five** sentences to write then insert a mix of **two tools** into each sentence. Underline the tools, and name their positions in parentheses: *opener, split, closer*. Before creating your tools, first learn more about the place or thing online so your tools will be informative and interesting.

1. The Model T Ford was the first car.

2. Thomas Edison invented the light bulb.

3. The Hope Diamond is the most famous jewel in the world.

4. Butterflies come from caterpillars.

5. Gutenberg's printing press made paper books possible.

6. Helicopters can do more than planes

7. The Constitution is the founding law of the United States of America.

8. New York City is one of the most popular tourist attractions in the world.

9. The *Titanic* ran into an iceberg.

10. Dumbo is a little flying elephant with big ears.

EXAMPLE OF MIXED TOOLS

1. *Opener and Split:* **A former senator from Illinois,** Barack Obama, **chosen as the democratic candidate,** was the first African American elected to the presidency of the United States.

2. *Split and Closer:* Barack Obama, **a graduate of Harvard Law School,** was the first African American elected to the presidency of the United States, **his presidency consisting of two terms in the White House from 2009 to 2017.**

3. *Opener and Closer:* **A recipient of the Nobel Peace Prize in 2009,** Barack Obama was the first African American elected to the presidency of the United States, **honored for many consecutive years as the most admired man in America.**

You did it! You got started with sentence composing, stayed the course, and crossed the finish line. You learned that in building sentences, the right tool in the right place gets the job done right.

No longer a sentence novice, you are now a sentence architect and builder. Congratulations!

THE SENTENCE-COMPOSING APPROACH

My approach is to focus all my attention on the sentences—
try to get them as good and honest and interesting as I can.

—George Saunders, award-winning author

BECOMING A WRITER

Below is the ending of E. B. White's *Charlotte's Web*,
a beloved heartwarming but also heartbreaking story
of the friendship between a pig named Wilbur, who can talk,
and a spider named Charlotte, who can write.

It is not often that someone comes along
who is a true friend and a good writer.
Charlotte was both.

We hope that you have already learned to be a true friend,
and that *Getting Started with Elementary School Sentence Composing*
has helped you become a better writer.
We, the coauthors of this worktext, send you our best wishes
for success in friendship and in writing.
—Don and Jenny Killgallon

Drawing by Don Killgallon